Forest Resources of the Hoosier National Forest
2005

Christopher W. Woodall, Judith A. Perez, and Thomas R. Thake

About the Authors:

Christopher W. Woodall is a Research Forester in the Forest Inventory and Analysis program at the Northern Research Station, USDA Forest Service, St. Paul, MN.

Judith A. Perez is a Forest Planner on the Hoosier National Forest, USDA Forest Service, Bedford, IN.

Thomas R. Thake is a Silviculturalist on the Hoosier National Forest, USDA Forest Service, Bedford, IN.

Foreword

We would like to present to you the latest results of the inventory of forest land on the Hoosier National Forest, *Forest Resources of the Hoosier National Forest, 2005*. The Hoosier worked cooperatively with the Forest Inventory and Analysis program of the USDA Forest Service and the Indiana Department of Natural Resources to complete the inventory. The results show that the Hoosier has a higher percentage of forested land than the rest of Indiana. Forest land on the Hoosier provides abundant wildlife habitat, recreation, and watershed protection.

The species composition of the Hoosier represents a diverse and resilient forest ecosystem. Forest composition is dominated by white oaks; however, since the previous inventory maple, yellow-poplar, and red oaks have increased. On average, the Hoosier is an aging forest with slightly larger trees than the rest of Indiana.

The future oak forest is in question on the Hoosier. Currently, there is insufficient oak regeneration here, allowing species such as maples, ashes, elms, and sassafras to replace the older oaks at a faster rate. This shift in forest composition could have implications for many of the wildlife species that use the Hoosier. Hard mast (e.g., acorns) provide important fall and winter food for much of the wildlife here.

It is difficult to develop adequate amounts of wildlife habitat on such a small land area that is interspersed with private lands. The area of the Hoosier that provides quality early successional habitat is relatively small compared to other areas in the State. Additionally, only a small percentage of the forested lands on the Hoosier meet the minimum requirements for Indiana bat roost habitat.

The Hoosier is a mature, healthy forest; however, threats still exist. Invasive species, pests/disease, fragmentation, and loss of early successional habitat are issues that need to be addressed. This report provides the public with a common set of statistically accurate numbers that can be used in land management decisionmaking.

We invite you to read through the information provided in *Forest Resources of the Hoosier National Forest, 2005*.

Kenneth G. Day
Forest Supervisor
Hoosier National Forest

Contents

Introduction

The Hoosier National Forest (Hoosier) comprises an estimated 200,000 acres in nine counties across southern Indiana (Fig. 1). The Hoosier was established by proclamation in 1935 and became a national forest in 1954. By the 1950s, more than 100 years of exploitive timber extraction, land clearing, and agricultural practices had severely degraded the hills, gently rolling plains, and bottomlands that currently make up the Hoosier. Today, the Hoosier is nearly fully occupied by a healthy and mature hardwood forest providing a wide array of resources for the citizens of the United States.

Figure 1. The Hoosier National Forest boundaries and lands, southern Indiana, 2005.

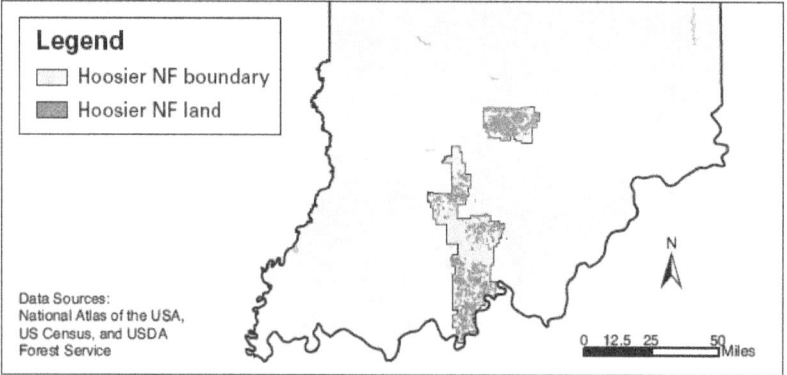

The Forest Inventory and Analysis (FIA) program of the USDA Forest Service is charged with inventorying and reporting on all forest land in the United States. FIA's first analysis of the Hoosier was based on a periodic inventory completed in 1998 (Leatherberry 2003). FIA now conducts an annual inventory in Indiana that allows reporting of the Hoosier's forest resources on a short timeframe (e.g., 5 years). The annual inventory includes the monitoring of the Hoosier's forest ecosystem attributes and responses to forest health issues and forest stand dynamics.

The Hoosier does not exist as an intact island within the surrounding forests of Indiana; rather, it is a forest ecosystem intermixed with private forest in a State that depends on its forest resources for its livelihood. Because the Hoosier makes up much of the public forest land in Indiana, it plays a major role in maintaining forest ecosystems that enhance biological diversity in the region and provides high-quality recreation opportunities. Management for large, contiguous, and natural forest ecosystems that contain native plant and animal communities provides a level of biological, genetic, and ecological process diversity not found in most areas of the State.

In this report, the forest resources of the Hoosier will be compared to the forest attributes in two additional reporting areas: the Greater Hoosier Community (GHC) and the entire State of Indiana. The GHC is non-federally owned land in the nine counties in which the Hoosier exists (Brown, Crawford, Dubois, Jackson, Lawrence, Martin, Monroe, Orange, and Perry) (Fig. 2). The State of Indiana reporting area is defined as all the non-federally owned land in Indiana.

Figure 2. Inventory reporting areas: State of Indiana, Greater Hoosier Community, and Hoosier National Forest.

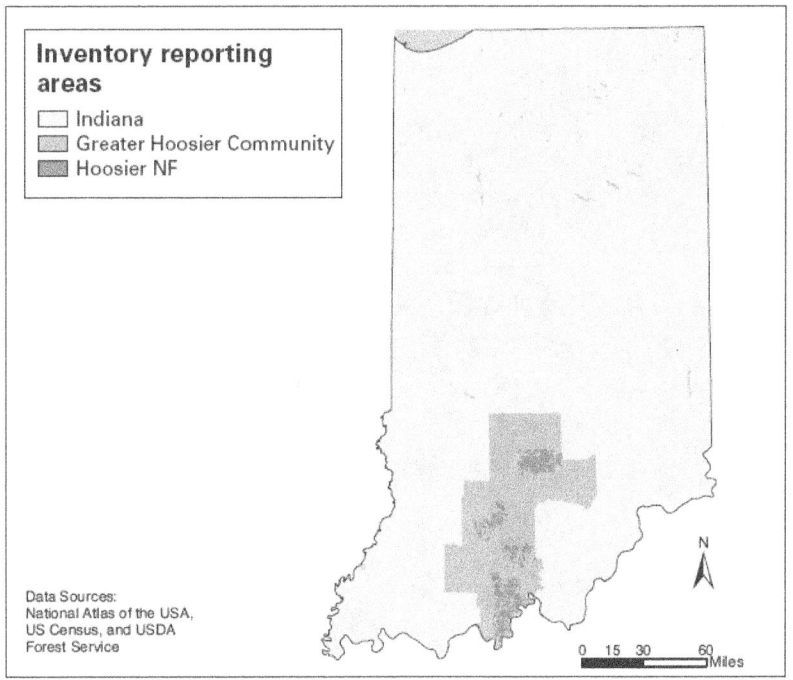

Highlights

- Over the past few decades the amount of forest land in the Hoosier has increased steadily and is currently estimated at more than 200,000 acres.

- The percentage of land within the Hoosier covered by forests is nearly five times that of the rest of Indiana.

- The aboveground dry biomass of trees in the Hoosier has increased by nearly 50 percent in the last 20 years.

- The total volume of sawtimber on the Hoosier has nearly doubled in the past 20 years.

- Compared to forests in the rest of Indiana and the GHC, the Hoosier has higher average tree biomass per acre and sawtimber volume per acre.

- The Hoosier is currently dominated by oaks, maples, and hickories.

- Of the tree species on the Hoosier, maples, red oaks, and yellow-poplars have had some of the largest increases in live-tree biomass during the last two decades.

- Most of the forest stands in the Hoosier are younger than 75 years, although older on average than forests across the rest of Indiana.

- The Hoosier has nearly 20 percent more trees per acre larger than 17 inches in diameter than the rest of Indiana.

- The average annual net growth on forest land of the Hoosier is less than forests across the rest of Indiana and is dominated by select white oaks.

- The Hoosier has over seven times more annual tree volume growth than mortality.

- Most mortality on the Hoosier is represented by the other red oaks species group.

- The regeneration of oaks in oak forest types is sparse, indicating the possible loss of oak forests in the future on the Hoosier.

- Compared to forests in the rest of Indiana and the surrounding non-Federal forest land, the Hoosier has a greater percentage of forest land with Indiana bat roost habitat.

Context of the Hoosier National Forest

Let's compare several features of the Hoosier with those of non-Federal forests surrounding the national forest (Greater Hoosier Community) and all non-Federal forests in the State of Indiana (the horizontal lines at the end of the bars represent the sampling errors, where available).

Live tree biomass per forest land acre:

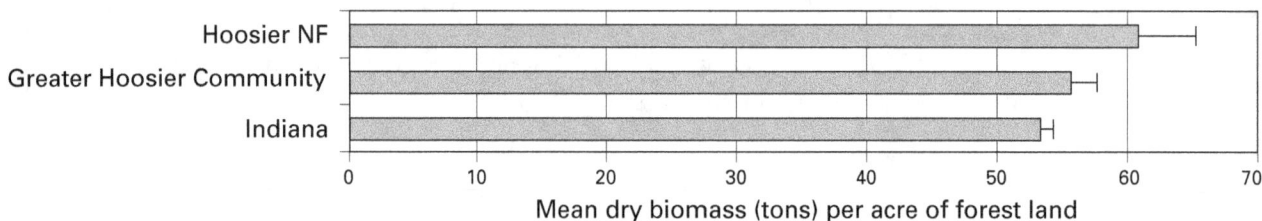

Tree volume growth per timberland acre:

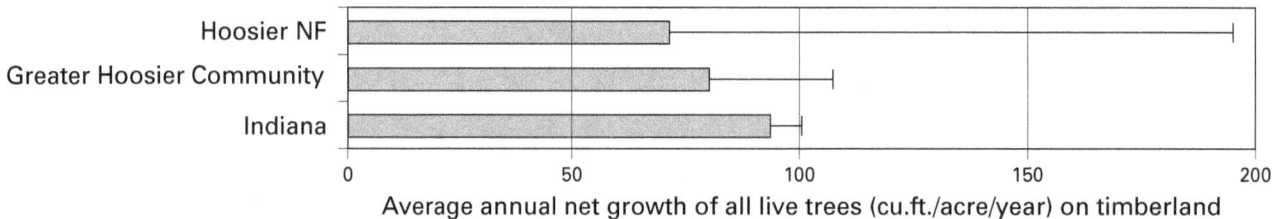

Tree volume mortality per timberland acre:

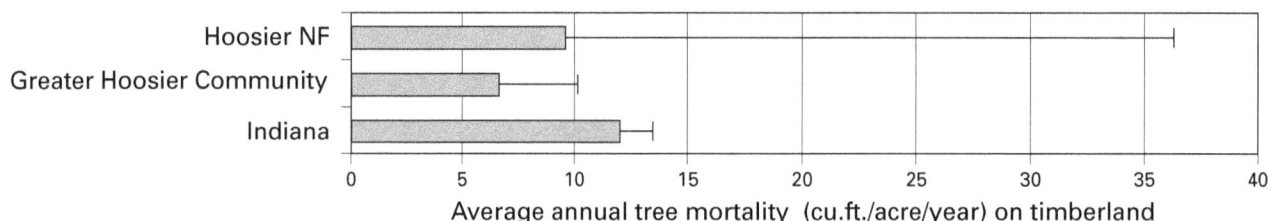

Number of oak seedlings per acre in oak forests:

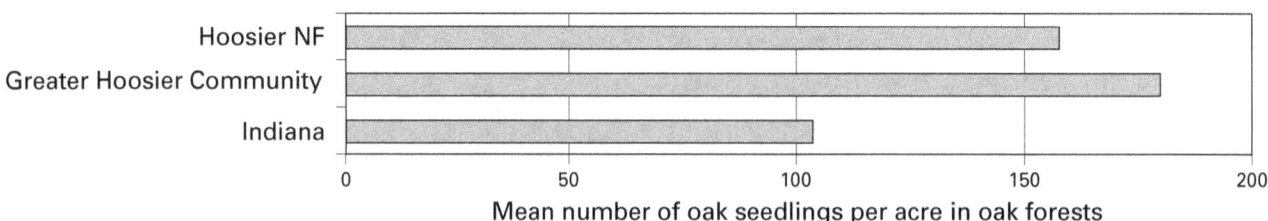

Number of trees smaller than 3 inches in diameter per forest land acre:

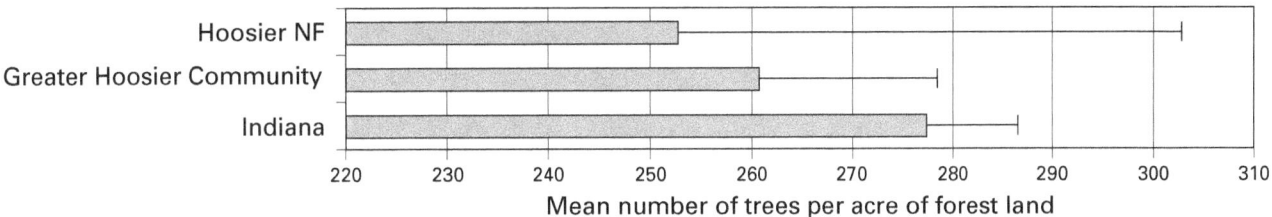

Mean number of trees per acre of forest land

Number of trees larger than 18 inches in diameter per forest land acre:

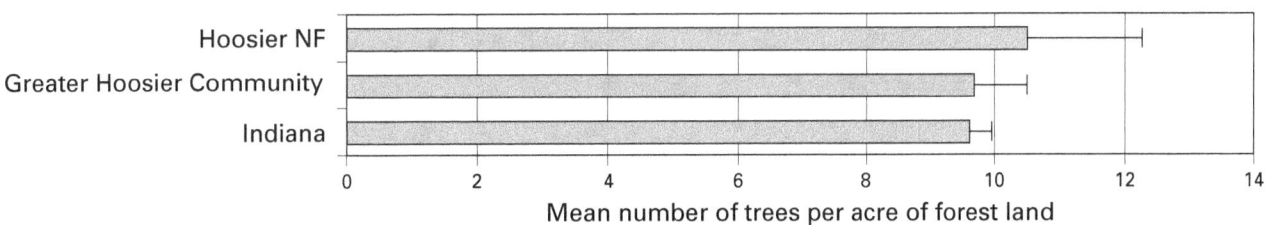

Mean number of trees per acre of forest land

Tree volume harvested per timberland acre:

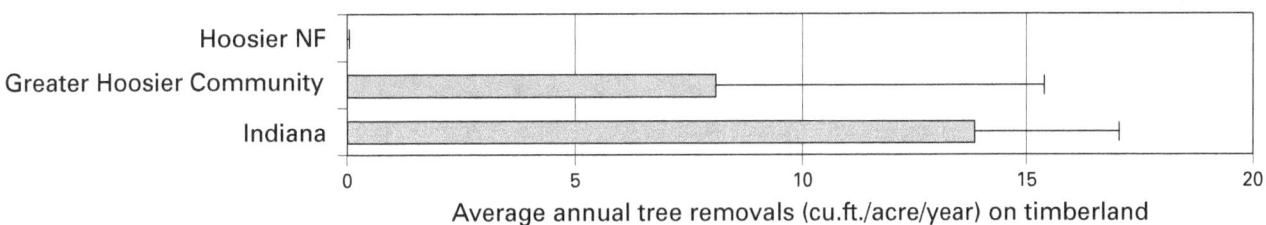

Average annual tree removals (cu.ft./acre/year) on timberland

Standing dead tree volume per forest land acre:

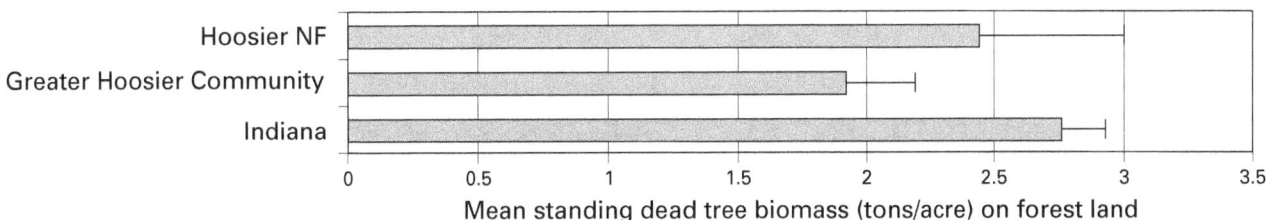

Mean standing dead tree biomass (tons/acre) on forest land

Features of the Hoosier National Forest

Forest Land Area

Background:

Quantifying the amount of land occupied by forests in the Hoosier is crucial to assessing the current status and trends in the forest ecosystem, along with the impact of forest land acquisitions. Fluctuations in the forest land base may also indicate changing land use trends and forest health conditions.

What We Found:

The area of forest land in the Hoosier has been steadily increasing since the first inventory in 1968 because of land purchases and conversion (Fig. 3). Forest land acreage estimates successively increased from 178,400 to 185,965 to 205,589 to 200,678 in years 1986, 1998, 2003, and 2005, respectively. Compared to the rest of Indiana and the Greater Hoosier Community (GHC), the Hoosier has a high proportion of forest land relative to total land area. Indiana is nearly 20 percent forested, the Greater Hoosier Community is more than 40 percent forested, and the Hoosier is more than 96 percent forested (Fig. 4). During the last 20 years, total forest land acreage has increased by more than 12 percent on the Hoosier compared to more than six percent for the State of Indiana and around one percent for the GHC (Fig. 5).

What This Means:

The forest land area in the Hoosier has been increasing for decades at a rate greater than that for the State of Indiana. However, this rate of increase is due to maturation/expansion of forest and land acquisition by the Hoosier. Additionally, the Hoosier exists in stark contrast to the rest of the land in the State and GHC in that nearly the entire land base is forested. Non-Federal lands near the national forest have had a forest land increase of only one percent during the past two decades, maintaining a rather stable forest land base. While the heavily forested land base of the Hoosier denotes a valuable natural resource, it also underscores the uniqueness of the national forest in the context of the State's entire resource base.

Figure 3. Area of forest land by inventory reporting years, 1986, 1998, 2003, and 2005, Hoosier National Forest, Indiana. (Note: 1967 estimate is for timberland area). The vertical lines at the data points represent the sample error associated with each inventory.

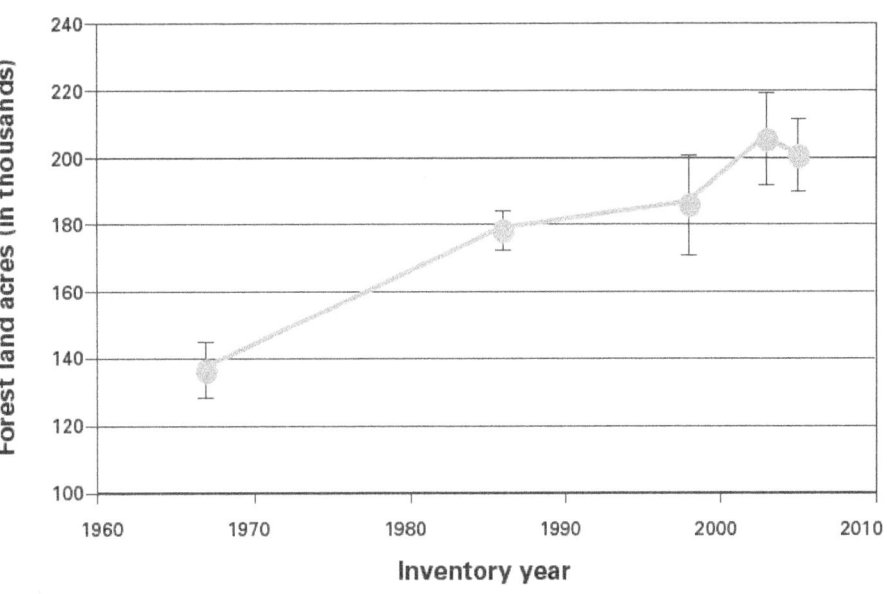

Figure 4. Percentage of total land area (including census water) that is forested by reporting area: State of Indiana, Greater Hoosier Community, and the Hoosier National Forest, 2001-2005. The vertical lines at the data points represent the sample error associated with each inventory.

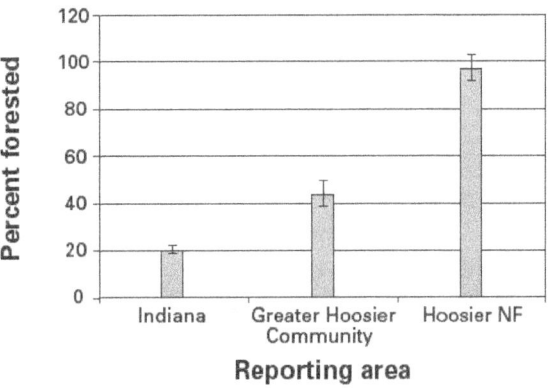

Figure 5. Percent change in area of forest land area between 1986 and 2005: State of Indiana, Greater Hoosier Community, and the Hoosier National Forest. The vertical lines at the data points represent the sample error associated with each inventory.

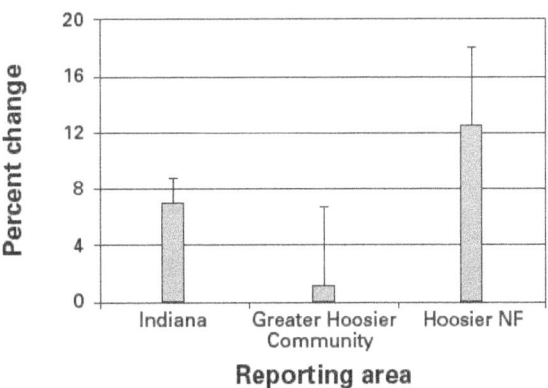

Biomass

Background:

Together with measures of Indiana's forest acreage, estimates of total biomass and its distribution among stand components indicates forest health trends and sustainability of forest management activities.

What We Found:

The biomass of all live trees on the Hoosier was estimated at more than 12 million dry tons in 2005 (Fig. 6). The Hoosier has steadily increased total live-tree biomass since the 1980s. It now has more than 14 percent more live-tree biomass per acre of forest land on average than the rest of the forests in Indiana (Fig. 7). The average acre of forest in the Hoosier has more than 60 tons per acre of live-tree biomass.

What This Means:

The total live-tree biomass on the Hoosier is a tremendous resource for the citizens of Indiana and the United States both in terms of economic and environmental importance. Biomass has been increasing at a steady rate for decades on the forest and is higher on average than in the rest of the forests in Indiana and the forests in the GHC. The carbon stored in the total live-tree biomass of the Hoosier approximately offsets the annual CO_2 emissions from more than 700,000 cars.

Figure 6. Total aboveground dry biomass of trees on forest land, Hoosier National Forest, 1986, 1998, 2003, and 2005. The vertical lines at the data points represent the sample error associated with each inventory.

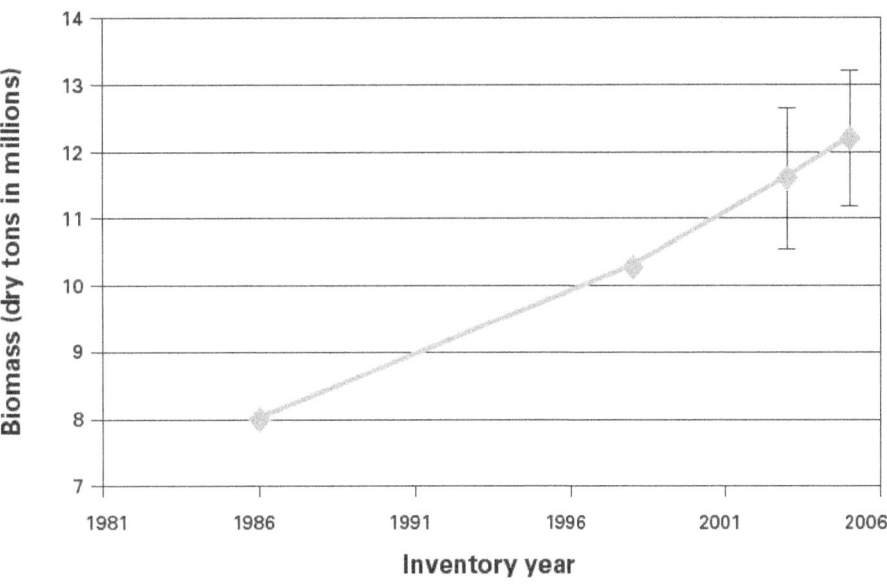

Figure 7. Mean dry biomass (tons) per acre for forest land, Indiana, the Greater Hoosier Community, and the Hoosier National Forest, 2001-2005. The vertical lines at the data points represent the sample error associated with each inventory.

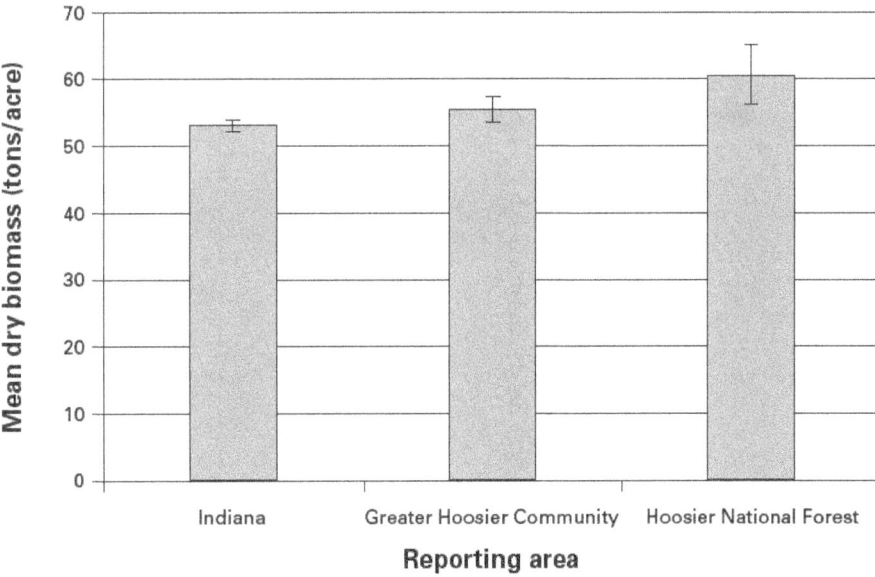

Sawtimber Volume

Background:

The quantity and quality of sawtimber volume on the Hoosier is an indicator of the economic value of the forest. Sawtimber volumes are a renewable natural resource of value to all citizens.

What We Found:

The total merchantable sawtimber volume (International 1/4-inch rule) on timberland in the Hoosier has increased steadily in the past decades to a current estimate of nearly 1.6 billion board feet (Fig. 8). It would take Indiana's mills approximately three years to process all this sawtimber if harvested. On a per acre of timberland basis, the Hoosier has 25 percent more merchantable sawtimber volume than the rest of Indiana and nearly 18 percent more than the GHC (Fig. 9). However, only 30 percent of Hoosier's sawtimber volume is in grades 1 and 2 (highest quality) compared to nearly 50 percent in those grades for the rest of sawtimber across Indiana (Fig. 10).

What This Means:

The Hoosier contains a wealth of sawtimber volume but of relatively poor grades. Because of multi-resource stewardship, the management of the Hoosier has not been focused on increasing sawtimber quality. Nonetheless, the absolute volume of sawtimber continues to increase on the Hoosier and will continue to appreciate as an asset for Indiana's citizens.

Figure 8. Total sawtimber (merchantable board foot volume) on timberland, Hoosier National Forest (1986, 1998, 2003, and 2005). The vertical lines at the data points represent the sample error associated with each inventory.

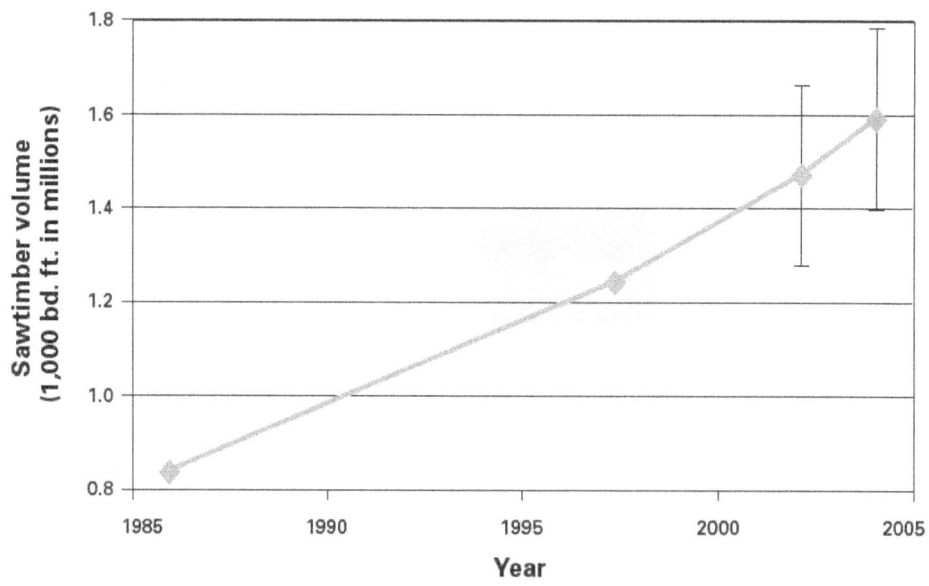

Figure 9. Average sawtimber volume per acre of timberland, Indiana, the Greater Hoosier Community, and the Hoosier National Forest, 2001-2005. The vertical lines at the data points represent the sample error associated with each inventory.

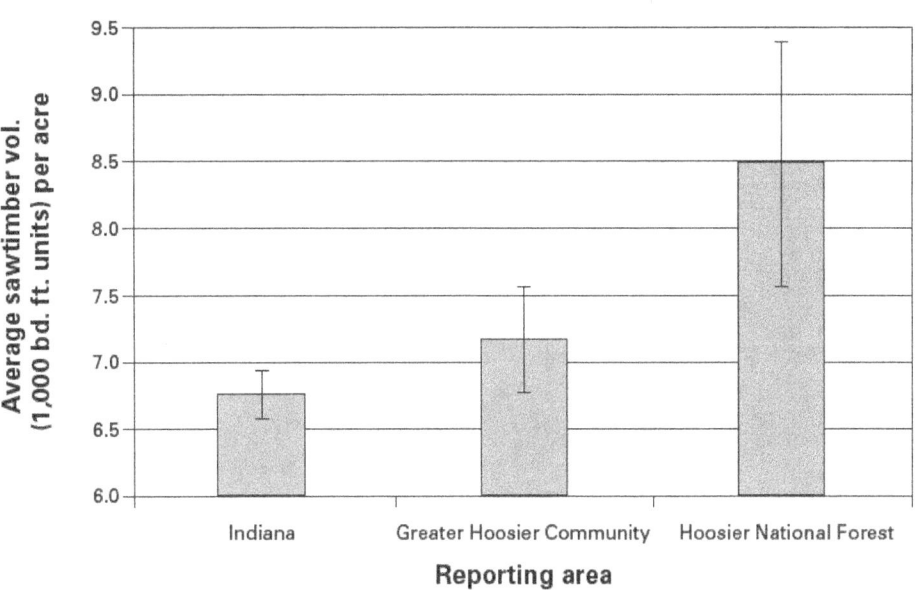

Figure 10. Distribution of sawtimber grade by board foot volume, Hoosier National Forest, 2001-2005.

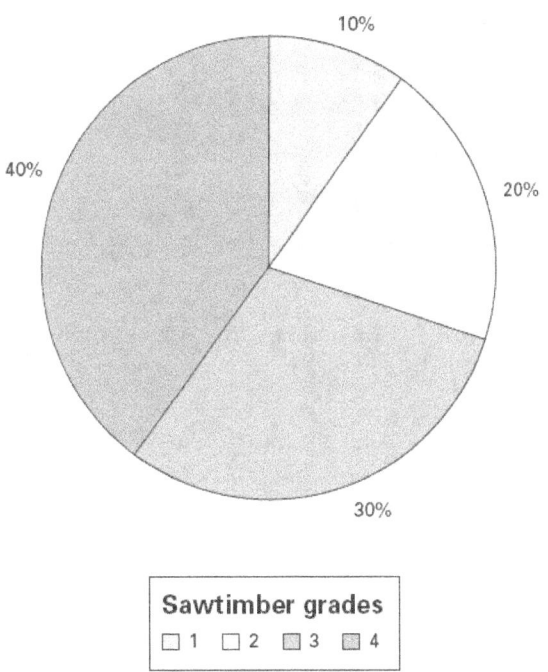

Species Composition

Background:

The species composition of a forest stand determines the dynamics of its growth, development, and ecosystem function. By looking at the current species composition and analyzing trends we can quantify the current and potential forest ecosystem character.

What We Found:

The tree species group with the largest amount of live biomass on the Hoosier was select white oaks at nearly three million tons of biomass (Fig. 11) (see Woodall et al. 2006 for species group definitions). The Hoosier has nearly 25 percent of its biomass in select white oaks while the GHC has a little over 15 percent and the rest of Indiana has 10 percent (Fig. 12). Other red oaks, hard maples, and hickory were also notable. Taken together, the maples were the second most prevalent species on the Hoosier in terms of biomass. The Hoosier has a lower percentage of hickory, yellow-poplar, and hard maple biomass than forests surrounding the Hoosier. Since 1986, the Hoosier has had tremendous increases in live-tree biomass (in excess of 100 percent) for maples, yellow-poplars, and select red oaks (Fig. 13).

What This Means:

The Hoosier is occupied by dozens of tree species representing a diverse and resilient forest ecosystem. However, a few tree species occupy the majority of live-tree biomass on the forest, most notably oaks, maples, and hickories. The Hoosier's tree species composition roughly follows the distribution of tree species in the GHC and the State of Indiana. The Hoosier has a bigger percentage of select white oaks than the rest of the State most likely due to a lack of harvesting and the longevity of white oaks. Given that maples, red oaks, and yellow-poplars have been showing the greatest increase in biomass since 1986, the species composition on the Hoosier may be expected to shift toward these species groups in the future.

Figure 11. Total live-tree biomass by species groups, Hoosier National Forest, 2001-2005. The horizontal lines at the end of the bars represent sampling errors.

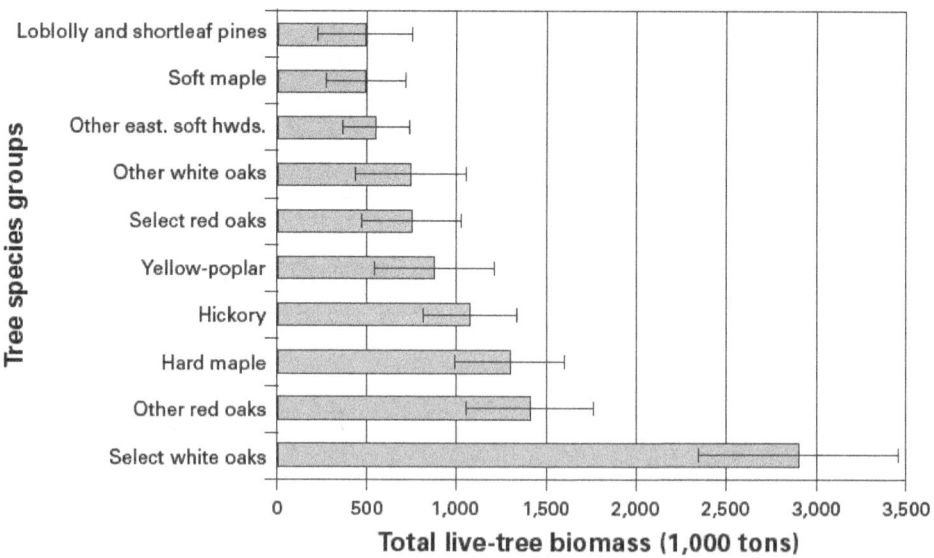

Figure 12. Percent of total live-tree biomass by selected species groups, Hoosier National Forest, Greater Hoosier Community, and Indiana, 2001-2005.

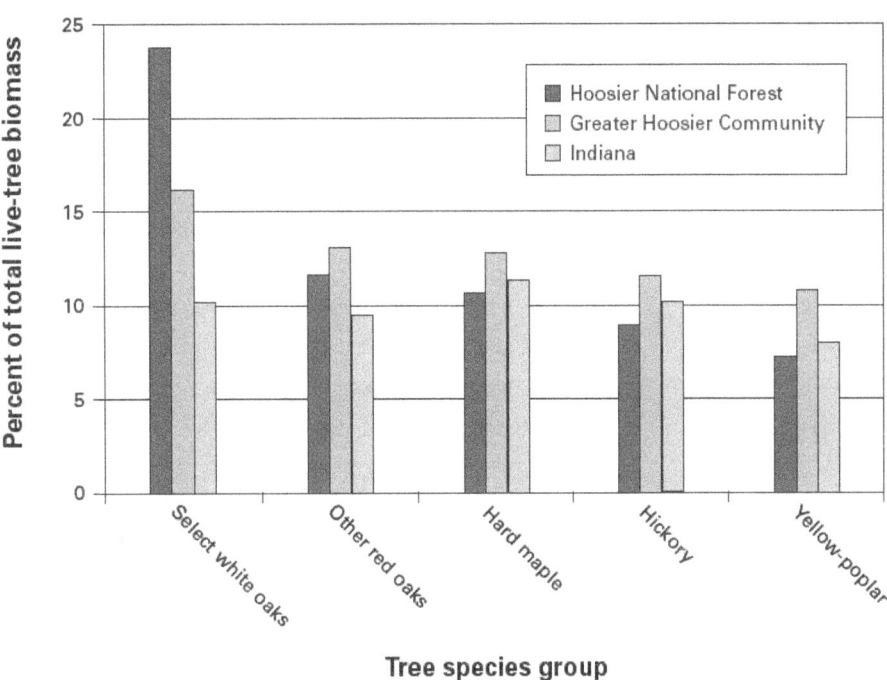

Figure 13. Percent increase in total live-tree biomass for selected tree species groups, Hoosier National Forest, 1986-2005.

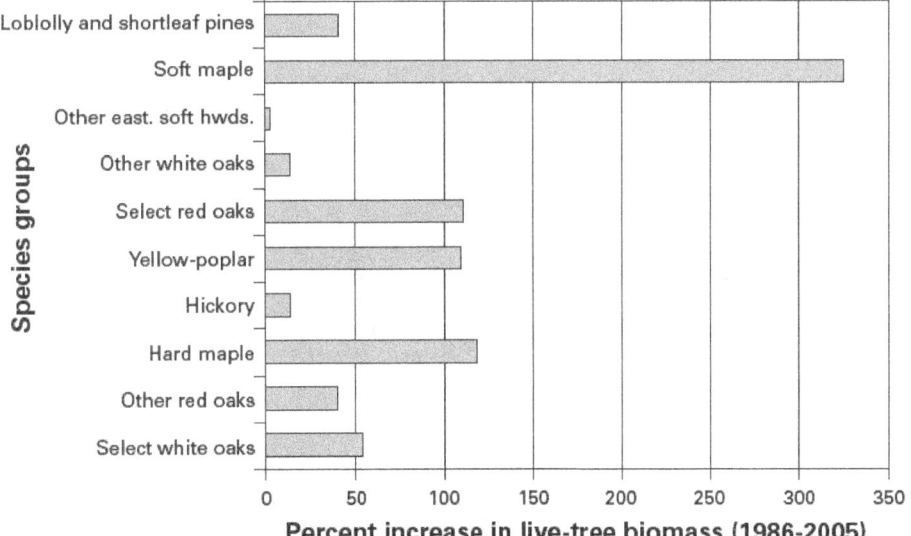

Tree Age and Size

Background:

The relationship between a tree's diameter and its age is critical in assessing growth rates and stages of stand development across forest conditions. Widespread declines in diameter/age relationships may indicate forest stands in later stages of stand development or succumbing to poor forest health.

What We Found:

Most of the Hoosier is older than 50 years (77 percent) (Fig. 14). Most notably, more than 30 percent of the forest in the Hoosier exceeds 75 years in age. In stark contrast, most forests in Indiana, excluding the Hoosier, are younger than 75 years (81 percent) and only 18 percent of forests are older than 75 years. The age of forests in the GHC is roughly between the older forests of the Hoosier and the State of Indiana. Despite differences in age distributions, there were fewer differences in the size-class distributions between the reporting areas. There was a "reverse-J" shaped distribution for all forests, with forests averaging nearly 350 trees per acre in the 1.0- to 4.9-inch size class and nearly 14 trees per acre in the 17.0-plus-inch size class (Fig. 15). However, the Hoosier had nearly 20 percent more trees in the largest size class compared to the rest of Indiana.

What This Means:

The Hoosier is on average older with slightly larger trees than the rest of Indiana, including forests immediately surrounding the Hoosier. The inventory did not record any stands over 125 years in age, either in the Hoosier or in the GHC. We can infer that although stands keep increasing in age and density, they are still not exceedingly old or do they possess size-

class distributions typical of older even-aged stands. More likely, most of the Hoosier is occupied by stands with a diversity of tree sizes in later stages of stand development given the advanced ages but "reverse-J" shaped size-class distribution. We can assume that without disturbance the forests of the Hoosier will continue to age with fewer small trees.

Steven Katovich, USDA Fo est Se vice, Bugwood o g

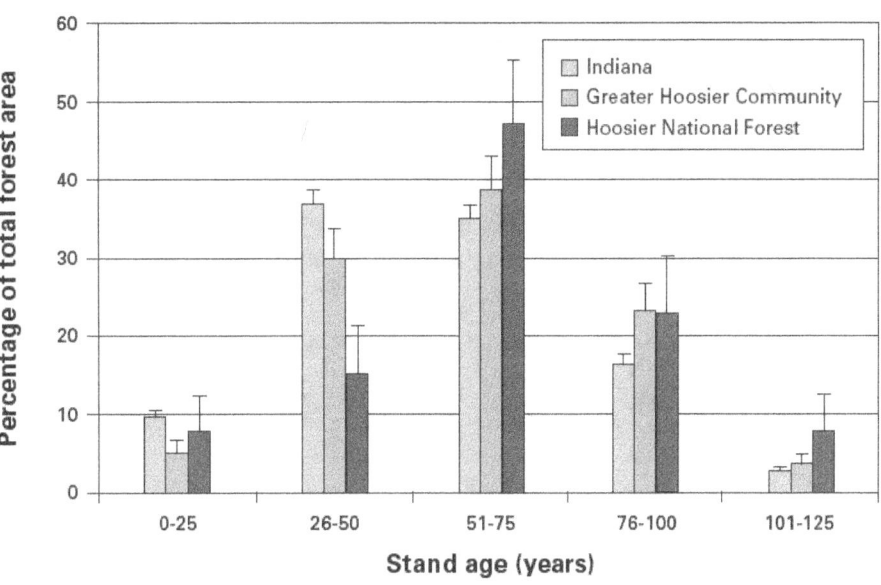

Figure 14. Percentage of total forest land area by stand-age class, Indiana, the Greater Hoosier Community, and the Hoosier National Forest, 2001-2005. The vertical lines at the data points represent the sample error associated with each inventory.

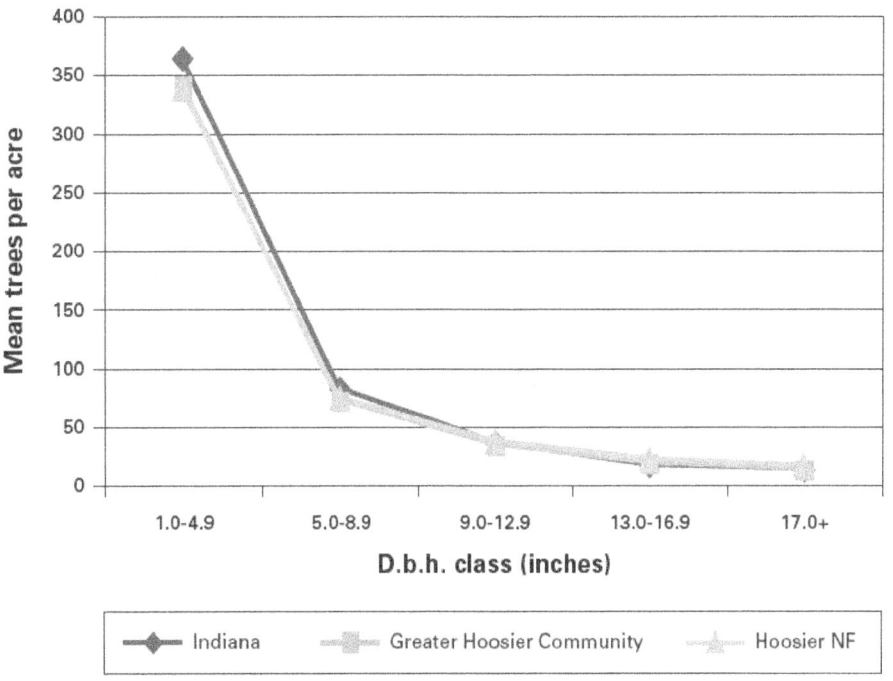

Figure 15. Mean trees per acre by tree diameter class for forest land, Indiana, the Greater Hoosier Community, and the Hoosier National Forest, 2001-2005.

Growth

Background:

Examining the net growth of forest ecosystem components may help us see the direction of forest succession/disturbance trends, accretion of forest resources, and vitality of various species groups.

What We Found:

The average annual net growth on forest land was nearly 70 cubic feet per acre per year in the Hoosier (Fig. 16), which was lower than that for forest land in the GHC (80 cubic feet) and in the rest of Indiana (94 cubic feet). Compared to the Hoosier NF, the average annual net growth was 36 percent greater on all other forest land in Indiana and 15 percent greater on forest land in the GHC. The biggest share of average annual net live-tree growth in the Hoosier was made up of the select white oaks species group at 38 percent of total growth (Fig. 17). Other species groups that contributed substantially to total growth on the Hoosier were other eastern soft hardwoods (11 percent), hickory (nine percent), other red oaks (nine percent), and hard maple (nine percent).

What This Means:

Given the advanced stand ages and late successional stages of stands within the Hoosier, average annual growth is less than that found in forests outside the national forest in Indiana. The annual growth is dominated by the tree species that have also dominated the species composition of the forest for decades: white and red oaks, hickory, and maples. Without substantial disturbance, the annual growth is expected to continue to decline as older trees senesce. Given the heavily forested condition of land within the Hoosier and some of the highest tree volumes in the State, annual growth would be expected to increase only if harvesting were to occur or if the oak/hickory components were to give way to maples and yellow-poplar through natural mortality and tree competition.

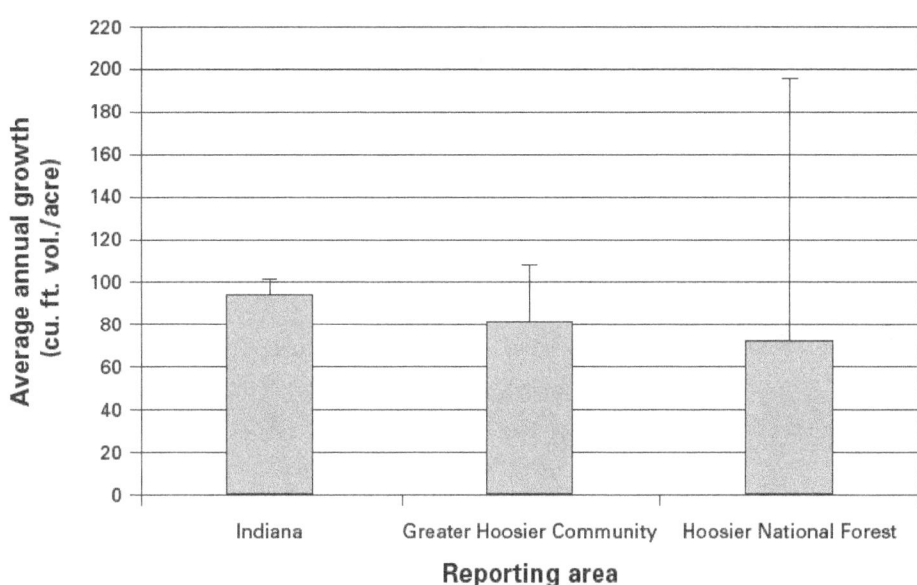

Figure 16. Average annual live-tree growth per acre on timberland, Indiana, Greater Hoosier Community, and the Hoosier National Forest, 1999 and 2000 to 2004 and 2005. The vertical lines at the data points represent the sample error associated with each inventory.

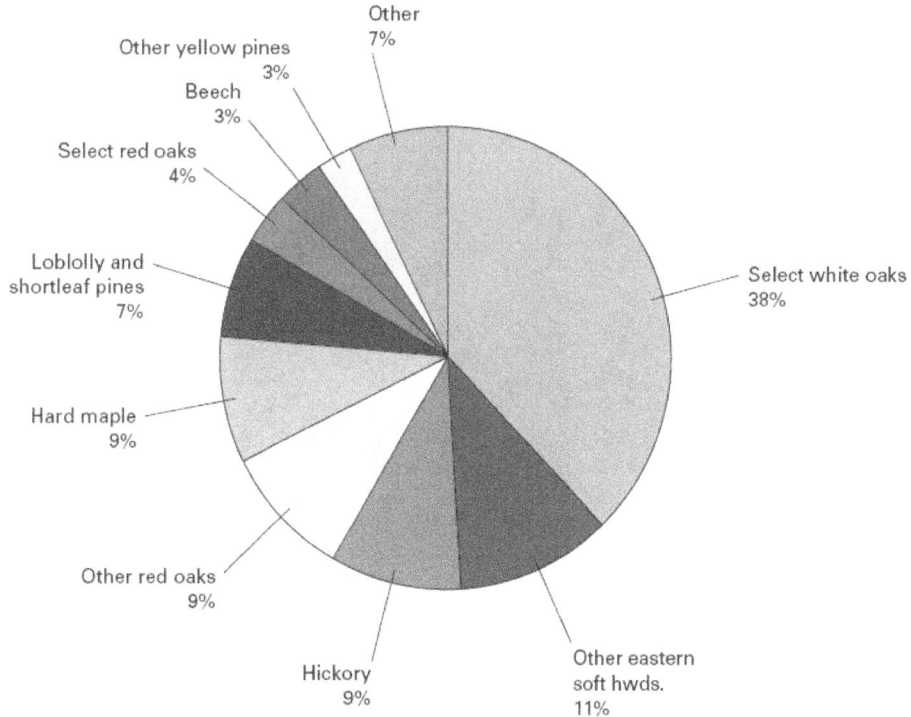

Figure 17. Percentage of total average annual live-tree growth by individual species groups, Hoosier National Forest, 1999-2000 to 2004-2005.

Mortality

Background:

Mortality is an important component of trends in forest resource accretion or depletion. Mortality may be attributed to the natural process of stand development, to attacks from forest pests (both native and exotic/invasive), and to stress from a combination of biotic (insects, fungi, and plants) and abiotic agents (air pollution and drought). Therefore, mortality is a natural component of a forest. A forest is defined as unhealthy when its mortality exceeds its capacity to respond (resiliency in terms of growth and regeneration).

What We Found:

The Hoosier averages approximately 9 cubic feet of mortality per forest land acre (Fig. 18). This rate of mortality is less than the nearly 12 cubic feet of mortality on forest land across Indiana and a little more than the 6 cubic feet of mortality in the GHC. Almost two-thirds (61 percent) of mortality was in the other red oak species group, followed by yellow-poplar (28 percent) and other eastern soft hardwoods (eight percent) (Fig. 19). The Hoosier has over seven times more annual tree volume growth than mortality.

What This Means:

The overall rates of tree mortality on the national forest are relatively low when compared to surrounding forests and to overall tree growth. This trend is likely to continue, barring a widespread onset of senescence in older forests or attacks from such insects and diseases such as emerald ash borer outbreak or sudden oak death. Although there is relatively low mortality, most of the tree mortality is in the other red oaks species group, a further indication of aging oak forest communities in the national forest.

Figure 18. Average annual live-tree mortality per acre on timberland, Indiana, Greater Hoosier Community, and the Hoosier National Forest, 1999-2000 to 2004-2005. The vertical lines at the data points represent the sample error associated with each inventory.

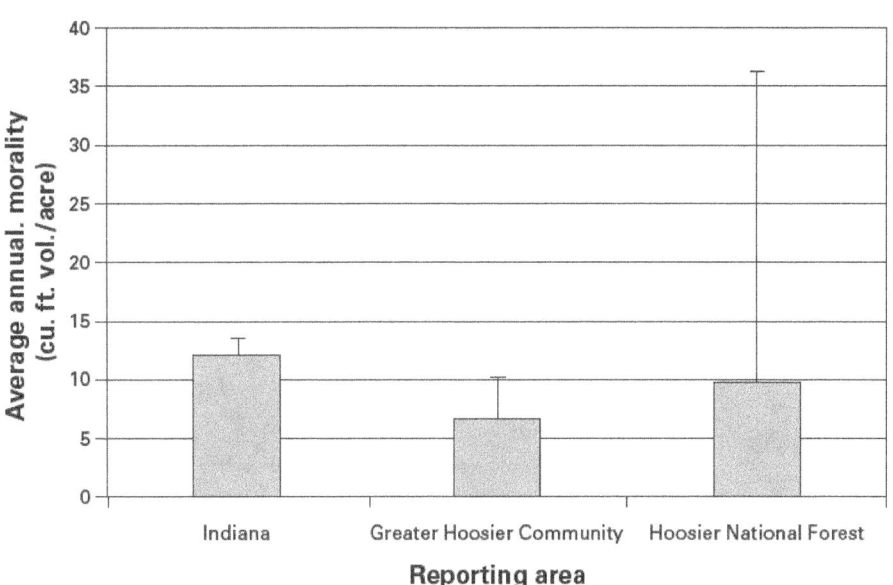

Figure 19. Percentage of total average annual live-tree mortality by individual species groups, Hoosier National Forest, by individual species groups between 1999-2000 and 2004-2005.

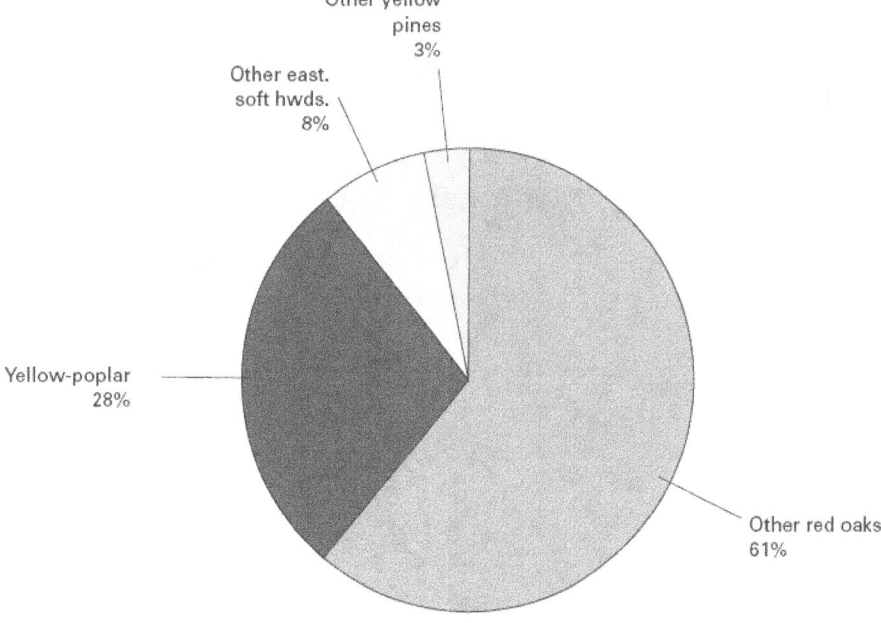

Removals

Background:

Data on the quantity of growing stock removed from timberland by human means indicates both the level and impact of management/utilization activities. Because removals are observed on only a few of inventory plots, greater variances are associated with removal estimates as than with other variables such as mortality or timberland area.

What We Found:

No inventory plots in the Hoosier were impacted by harvest activities from 2004 to 2005. Thus, the estimate of removals on the national forest is zero, compared to the rest of Indiana (14 cubic feet per acre/year) and the GHC (8 cubic feet per acre/year) (Fig. 20). According to the cut and sold data collected by Hoosier staff, between 2002 and 2005 the Hoosier had an average annual removal rate of roughly 125 MBF per year or less than one ten-thousandth of all the sawtimber on Hoosier timberland (Fig. 21).

What This Means:

The rate of removals on the Hoosier is so low that a large-scale systematic inventory estimated an annual removal rate of zero. This value indicates a very low level of active vegetation manipulation and utilization on the Hoosier, most likely a fraction of the removal rate found in the GHC.

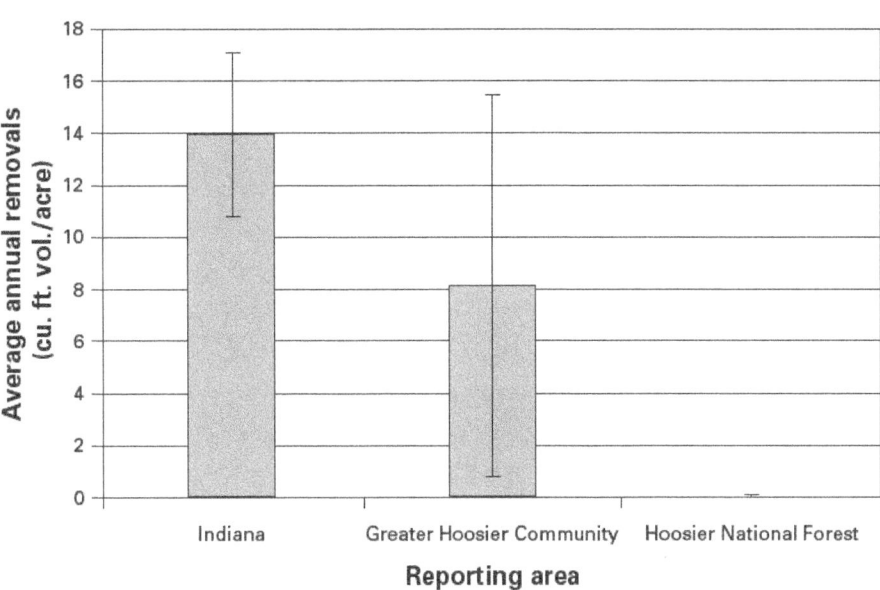

Figure 20. Average annual live-tree removals per acre of timberland, Indiana, Greater Hoosier Community, and the Hoosier National Forest, 1999-2000 to 2004-2005. The vertical lines at the data points represent the sample error associated with each inventory.

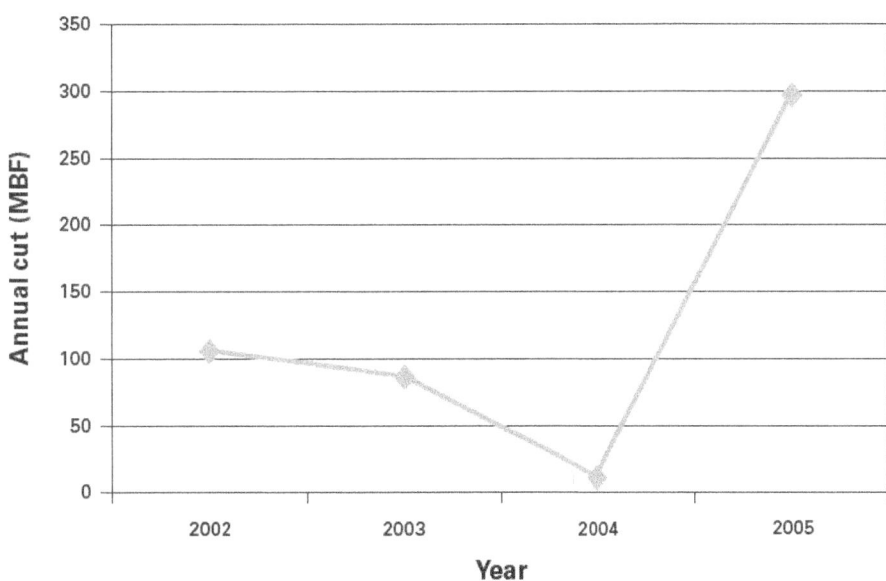

Figure 21. Annual cut on the Hoosier National Forest as estimated by the Hoosier National Forest, 2002-2005.

Oak Regeneration

Background:

Oak forest types have dominated the Hoosier for decades. Not only are oak trees a vital component of Indiana's hardwood industry, they also provide food and habitat to numerous wildlife species. Successful regeneration and survival of oak seedlings is critical to the future of the oak resource in the heart of Indiana's most heavily forested region.

What We Found:

Across Indiana, oak seedlings in oak forest types are sparse, regardless of ownership. The proportion of oak seedlings in oak forest types was approximately eight percent in Indiana's forests (Fig. 22). The proportions were also low in both the GHC and the Hoosier, a little above eight percent. If oak species don't constitute the majority of seedlings in oak forests in the national forest, which species do? The species groups of eastern noncommercial hardwoods, other eastern soft hardwoods, hard maple, and ash constitute nearly two-thirds of seedlings in oak forests (Fig. 23).

What This Means:

The future of oak forests is in doubt within the Hoosier. The low percentage of oak seedlings in current oak forests indicates insufficient establishment of younger oak trees to replace older, senescing ones. Without adequate oak regeneration to perpetuate the oaks, other tree species such as maples, ashes, elms, and sassafras are likely to eventually dominate former oak forests. This situation can be found across Indiana. However, given the multiple-use management policy of national forests, the ability to change the course of tree species shift by way of management is more limited in the Hoosier than in non-Federal forests. One beneficial outcome of senescing oak forests is the preponderance of large oak trees and snags providing habitat for numerous fauna in the years ahead.

Figure 22. Percent of tree seedlings in oak forests that are oak species, Indiana, Greater Hoosier Community, and the Hoosier National Forest, 2001-2005. The vertical lines at the data points represent the sample error associated with each inventory.

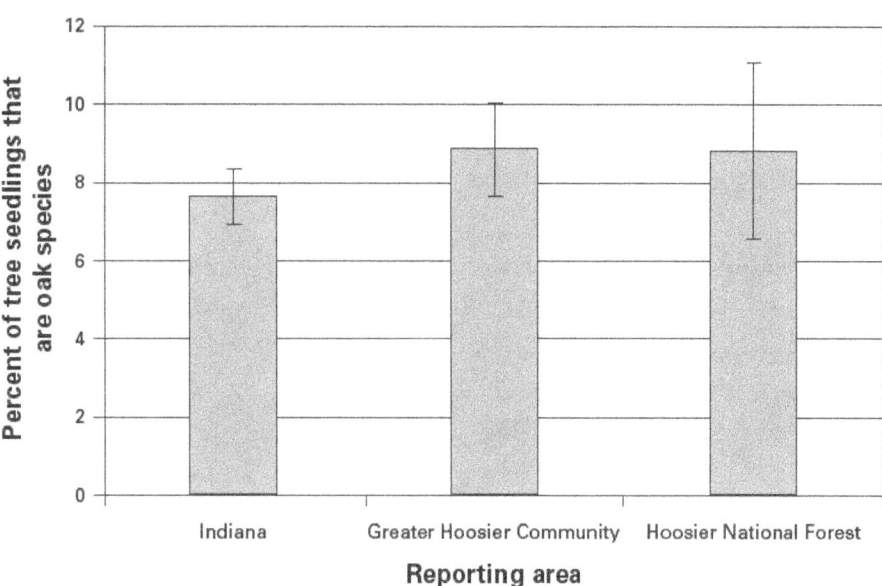

Figure 23. Average number of seedlings per acre of oak forest land, Hoosier National Forest, 2001-2005. The horizontal lines at the end of the bars represent sampling errors.

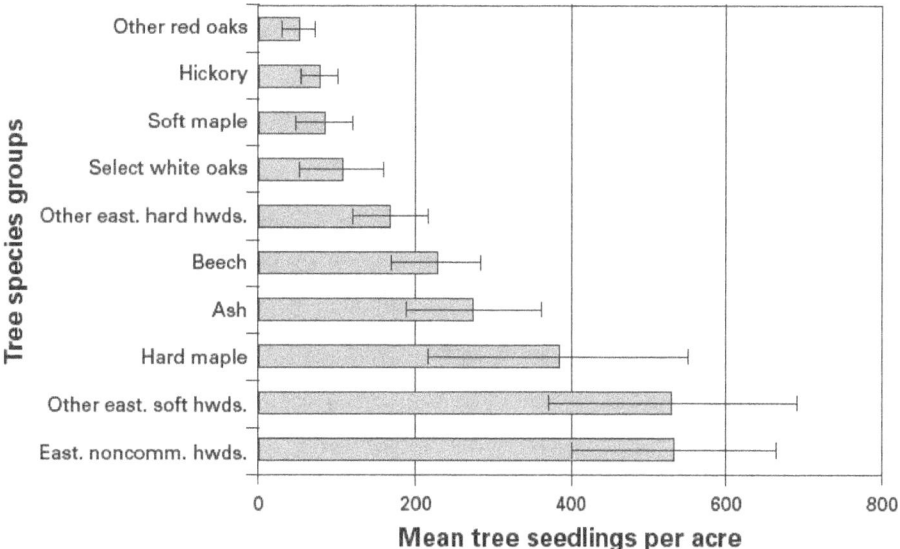

Wildlife Habitat

Background:

The type of habitat required by wildlife species in the Hoosier is highly variable, depending on the wildlife species themselves. Some species require the open stand structures and forage of early successional forests, while other species require the nesting habitat found in large trees in later successional stands.

What We Found:

Approximately eight percent of the Hoosier may be in an early successional stage (Fig. 24). An early successional stage is based on a stand with a mean live tree diameter less than 3 inches. Regardless of such threshold settings, the Hoosier has substantially fewer stands occupied by small trees than the rest of forests in Indiana and the GHC. Using the early successional criterion of this analysis, the State of Indiana has more than 14 percent of forests in early succession.

Nearly 30 percent of the Hoosier's forest land has at least the minimum required Indiana bat roost habitat (defined as at least three trees in excess of 20 inches in diameter of any of the following species: silver maple, bitternut/shellbark/shagbark hickory, white/green ash, cottonwood, white/northern red/post oak, black locust, or American/slippery elm; see USDA Forest 2006) (Fig. 25). The average number of trees per acre meeting the size requirements for Indiana bat roosts is 2.9 for the Hoosier (compared to the minimum required three). Only 20 percent of the forest land in the GHC has the required minimum Indiana bat roost habitat.

What This Means:

It is difficult to achieve adequate habitat requirements for diverse assemblages of species requiring diverse habitats, especially in relatively small land areas such as the Hoosier's 200,000 acres. For roosting habitat. Indiana bats require large trees found in late successional forests. This requirement may be attainable in the Hoosier because of its high density and mature forests. In contrast, given the mature forests there is a lack of early successional habitat. Simultaneous efforts to increase large-tree accretion and create more "young" forests may be mutually exclusive at small scales. Given the current status of forests on the Hoosier and lack of disturbance, we would expect Indiana bat habitat to increase and early successional habitat to decrease in the future.

Figure 24. Percent of forest land acreage in early succession (mean live-tree diameter less than 3 inches at breast height), Indiana, Greater Hoosier Community, and the Hoosier National Forest, 2005.

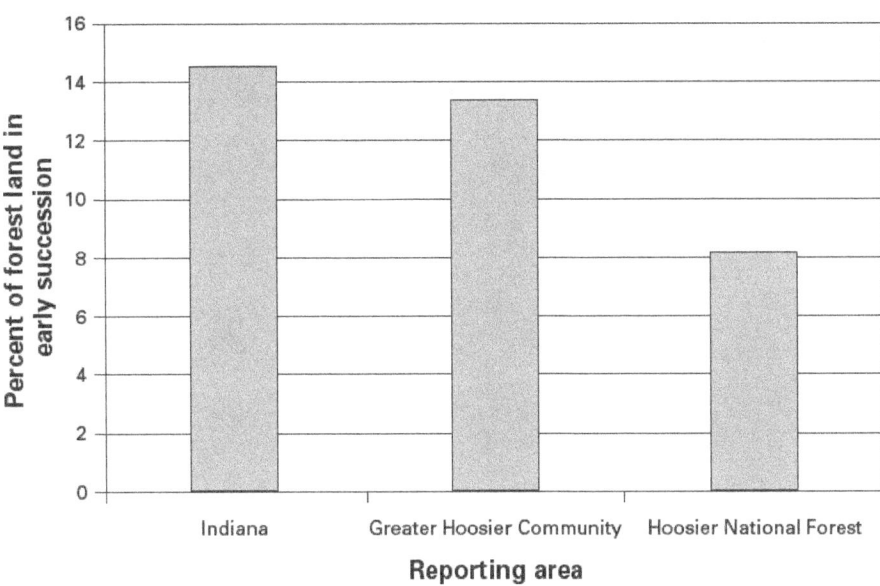

Figure 25. Percent of forest land area with Indiana bat roost habitat (three trees per acre meeting size and species criteria, USDA Forest Service 2006).

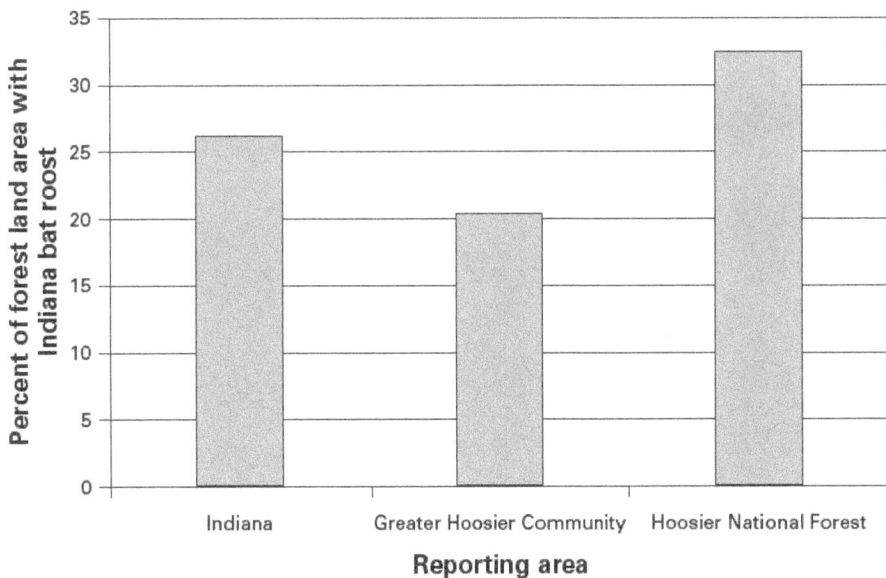

Data Sources and Techniques

Data Sources and Techniques

The North Central Research Station's Forest Inventory and Analysis (NCFIA) program began fieldwork for the fifth inventory of Indiana forest resources in 1999. (The North Central Station merged with the Northeastern Station in 2006 to form the Northern Research Station. NCFIA is now NFIA.) This inventory launched the new annual inventory system in which one-fifth of the field plots (considered one panel) in the State are measured each year. In 2003, NCFIA completed measurement of the fifth and final panel of annual inventory plots in Indiana (Woodall et al. 2005). In 2004, NCFIA began remeasuring annual inventory plots across Indiana. Previous inventories of Indiana's forest resources were completed in 1950, 1967, 1986, and 1998 (Hutchison 1956, Schmidt et al. 2000, Smith and Golitz 1988, Spencer 1969, Spencer et al. 1990, Woodall et al. 2005). A report on the previous inventory and analysis of the Hoosier NF was released in 2003 based on the last periodic inventory conducted in Indiana in 1998 (Leatherberry 2003).

Data from new inventories are often compared with data from earlier inventories to determine trends in forest resources. For the comparisons to be valid, the procedures used in inventories must be similar. Although these changes will have little impact on statewide estimates of forest area, timber volume, and tree biomass, they may significantly impact plot classification variables such as forest type and stand-size class. For estimating growth, removals, and mortality, the annual inventories in 1999 and 2000 were compared with plots remeasured in 2004 and 2005. With only 40 percent of inventory plots used to determine growth, removals, and mortality, only limited conclusions can be attributed to these estimates.

The Hoosier NF inventory was done in three phases. During the first phase, FIA used a computer-assisted classification of satellite imagery to form two initial strata—forest and nonforest. Pixels within 60 m (2 pixel widths) of a forest/nonforest edge formed two additional strata—forest/nonforest and nonforest/forest. Forest pixels within 60 m on the forest side of a forest/nonforest boundary were classified into a forest edge stratum. Pixels within 60 m of the boundary on the nonforest side were classified into a nonforest edge stratum. The estimated population total for a variable is the sum across all strata of the product of each stratum's estimated area and the variable's estimated mean per unit area for the stratum.

The second phase of the forest inventory measured the annual sample of field plots in Indiana. Current FIA precision standards for annual inventories require a sampling intensity of one plot for approximately every 6,000 acres. FIA has divided the entire area of the United States into nonoverlapping hexagons, each of which contains 5,937 acres (McRoberts 1999). The total Federal base sample of plots was systematically divided into five interpenetrating, nonoverlapping subsamples or panels. Each year the plots in a single panel are measured, and panels are selected on a 5-year, rotating basis. For estimation purposes, the measurement of each panel of plots may be considered an independent systematic sample of all land in a State. Field crews measure vegetation on plots forested at the time of the last inventory and on plots currently classified as forest by trained photointerpreters using aerial photos or digital orthoquads.

NCFIA has two categories of field plot measurements—phase 2 field plots (standard FIA plots) and phase 3 plots (forest health plots) to optimize our ability to collect data when available for measurement. A suite of tree and site attributes are measured on phase 2 plots, and a full suite of forest health variables are measured on phase 3 plots. Both types of plot are uniformly distributed both geographically and temporally. The 2001–2005 annual inventory results represent field measures on 982 phase 2 forested plots in Indiana, 172 phase 2 plots in the Greater Hoosier Community, and 62 phase 2 plots in the Hoosier NF (which had a double intensity sample of phase 2 plots: 3,000 acres per phase 2 plot times 62 plots roughly equals the forest area of the Hoosier). Sampling errors are estimated for numerous figures in this report, although their determination is not possible for older inventories or readily attainable for special analyses.

The overall phase 2 plot layout consists of four subplots. The centers of subplots 2, 3, and 4 are located 120 feet from the center of subplot 1. The azimuths to subplots 2, 3, and 4 are 0, 120, and 240 degrees, respectively. Trees with a d.b.h. 5 inches and larger are measured on a 24-foot-radius (1/24 acre) circular subplot. All trees less than 5 inches d.b.h. are measured on a 6.8-foot-radius (1/300 acre) circular microplot located 12 feet east of the center of each of the four subplots. Forest conditions that occur on any of the four subplots are recorded. Factors that differentiate forest conditions are changes in forest type, stand-size class, land use, ownership, and density. For details on the sample protocols for phase 2 variables and all phase 3 indicators, please refer to http://fia.fs.fed.us/library/fact-sheets/.

For further information on the inventory methods, overall Indiana analysis, and a glossary of terms, please refer to Woodall et al. (2005 and 2006).

Literature Cited

Hutchison, O.K. 1956. *Indiana's forest resources and industries.* For. Ser. Rep. 10. Washington, DC: U.S. Department of Agriculture, Forest Service. 44 p.

Leatherberry, E.C. 2003. *The forest resources of the Hoosier National Forest, 1998.* Resour. Bull. NC-210. St. Paul, MN: U.S. Department of Agriculture, Forest Service, North Central Research Station. 54 p.

McRoberts, R.E. 1999. *Joint annual forest inventory and monitoring system, the North Central perspective.* Journal of Forestry. 97(12): 27-31.

Schmidt, T.L.; Hansen, M.H.; Solomakos, J.A. 2000. *Indiana's forests in 1998.* Resour. Bull. NC-196. St. Paul, MN: U.S. Department of Agriculture, Forest Service, North Central Research Station. 139 p.

Smith, W.B.; Golitz, M.F. 1988. *Indiana forest statistics, 1986.* Resour. Bull. NC-108. St. Paul, MN: U.S. Department of Agriculture, Forest Service, North Central Forest Experiment Station. 39 p.

Spencer, J.S. 1969. *Indiana's timber.* Resour. Bull. NC-7. St. Paul, MN: U.S. Department of Agriculture, Forest Service, North Central Forest Experiment Station. 61 p.

Spencer, J.S.; Kingsley, N.P.; Mayer, R.V. 1990. *Indiana's timber resource, 1986: an analysis.* Resour. Bull. NC-113. St. Paul, MN: U.S. Department of Agriculture, Forest Service, North Central Forest Experiment Station. 85 p.

USDA Forest Service. 2006. *Final environmental impact statement, land and resource management plan, Hoosier National Forest.* Milwaukee, WI: U.S. Department of Agriculture, Forest Service, Eastern Region. 381 p.

Woodall, C.W.; Johnson, D.; Gallion, J.; Perry, C.H.; Butler, B.; Piva, R.; Jepsen, E.; Nowak, D.; Marshall, P. 2005. *Indiana's forests, 1999-2003. Part A.* Resour. Bull. NC-253A. St. Paul, MN: U.S. Department of Agriculture, Forest Service, North Central Research Station. 95 p.

Woodall, C.W.; Hansen, M.; Brand, G.; McRoberts, R.; Gallion, J.; Jepsen, E. 2006. *Indiana's forests, 1999-2003. Part B.* Resour. Bull. NC-253B. St. Paul, MN: U.S. Department of Agriculture, Forest Service, North Central Research Station. 85 p.

Appendix Tables

Table 1.—Area of land in wilderness, timberland, and other forest conditions, by forest type group and forest type, Hoosier National Forest, Indiana, 2001-2005

(In thousand acres)

Forest type group and forest type	Forested condition			All forest land
	Wilderness	Timberland	Other forest	
White / red / jack pine group				
Eastern white pine	- -	4.1	- -	4.1
Total	- -	4.1	- -	4.1
Loblolly / shortleaf pine group				
Shortleaf pine	- -	9.4	- -	9.4
Virginia pine	- -	0.7	- -	0.7
Total	- -	10.0	- -	10.0
Oak / pine group				
White pine / red oak / white ash	- -	5.7	- -	5.7
Eastern redcedar / hardwood	- -	1.4	- -	1.4
Shortleaf pine / oak	3.3	3.3	- -	6.5
Virginia pine / southern red oak	- -	2.1	- -	2.1
Total	3.3	12.4	- -	15.7
Oak / hickory group				
Chestnut oak	- -	7.3	- -	7.3
White oak / red oak / hickory	- -	76.1	- -	76.1
White oak	3.3	31.2	- -	34.4
Yellow-poplar / white oak / red oak	- -	2.9	- -	2.9
Scarlet oak	- -	3.3	- -	3.3
Yellow-poplar	- -	3.3	- -	3.3
Chestnut oak / black oak / scarlet oak	6.5	3.3	- -	9.8
Mixed upland hardwoods	- -	6.4	- -	6.4
Total	9.8	133.8	- -	143.5
Elm / ash / cottonwood group				
River birch / sycamore	- -	3.3	- -	3.3
Total	- -	3.3	- -	3.3
Maple / beech / birch group				
Sugar maple / beech / yellow birch	- -	20.7	- -	20.7
Cherry / ash / yellow-poplar	- -	3.5	- -	3.5
Total	- -	24.2	- -	24.2
All forest types	13.0	187.8	- -	200.8

All table cells without observations in the inventory sample are indicated by - -. Table value of 0.0 indicates the acres round to less than 0.1 thousand acres. Columns and rows may not add to their totals due to rounding.

Table 2.—Area of forest land by forest type group, forest type, and stand-size class, Hoosier National Forest, Indiana, 2001-2005

(in thousand acres)

Forest type group	Stand-size class					All size classes
	Large diameter	Medium diameter	Small diameter	Chaparral	Nonstocked	
White / red / jack pine group						
Eastern white pine	4.1	- -	- -	- -	- -	4.1
Total	4.1	- -	- -	- -	- -	4.1
Loblolly / shortleaf pine group						
Shortleaf pine	9.4	- -	- -	- -	- -	9.4
Virginia pine	0.7	- -	- -	- -	- -	0.7
Total	10.0	- -	- -	- -	- -	10.0
Oak / pine group						
White pine / red oak / white ash	5.7	- -	- -	- -	- -	5.7
Eastern redcedar / hardwood	- -	1.4	- -	- -	- -	1.4
Shortleaf pine / oak	6.5	- -	- -	- -	- -	6.5
Virginia pine / southern red oak	- -	2.1	- -	- -	- -	2.1
Total	12.2	3.5	- -	- -	- -	15.7
Oak / hickory group						
Chestnut oak	7.3	- -	- -	- -	- -	7.3
White oak / red oak / hickory	69.7	3.6	2.8	- -	- -	76.1
White oak	34.4	- -	- -	- -	- -	34.4
Yellow-poplar / white oak / red oak	2.9	- -	- -	- -	- -	2.9
Scarlet oak	3.3	- -	- -	- -	- -	3.3
Yellow-poplar	0.1	3.3	- -	- -	- -	3.3
Chestnut oak / black oak / scarlet oak	9.8	- -	- -	- -	- -	9.8
Mixed upland hardwoods	- -	6.4	- -	- -	- -	6.4
Total	127.5	13.2	2.8	- -	- -	143.5
Elm / ash / cottonwood group						
River birch / sycamore	3.3	- -	- -	- -	- -	3.3
Total	3.3	- -	- -	- -	- -	3.3
Maple / beech / birch group						
Sugar maple / beech / yellow birch	18.9	1.8	- -	- -	- -	20.7
Cherry / ash / yellow-poplar	- -	- -	3.5	- -	- -	3.5
Total	18.9	1.8	3.5	- -	- -	24.2
All forest type groups	175.9	18.5	6.3	- -	- -	200.8

All table cells without observations in the inventory sample are indicated by - -. Table value of 0.0 indicates the acres round to less than 0.1 thousand acres. Columns and rows may not add to their totals due to rounding.

Table 3.—Number of all live trees on forest land by species, species group, and diameter class, Hoosier National Forest, Indiana, 2001-2005

(In thousand trees)

Species group	Diameter class (inches)															All classes
	1.0-2.9	3.0-4.9	5.0-6.9	7.0-8.9	9.0-10.9	11.0-12.9	13.0-14.9	15.0-16.9	17.0-18.9	19.0-20.9	21.0-24.9	25.0-28.9	29.0-32.9	33.0-36.9	37.0+	
Loblolly and shortleaf pines																
shortleaf pine	--	--	137	274	313	274	215	196	98	--	--	--	--	--	--	1,507
Other yellow pines																
Virginia pine	--	--	137	157	39	--	--	--	--	--	--	--	--	--	--	333
Eastern white and red pines																
eastern white pine	--	975	313	313	157	235	39	78	59	--	20	--	--	--	--	2,188
Other eastern softwoods																
eastern redcedar	487	975	489	354	78	39	59	20	20	--	--	--	--	--	--	2,520
Select white oaks																
white oak	1,706	731	391	592	393	470	453	571	352	157	254	78	--	--	--	6,168
chinkapin oak	244	--	78	40	20	39	--	--	40	--	--	--	--	--	--	462
Select red oaks																
northern red oak	731	--	99	39	78	59	59	59	98	59	59	59	--	--	--	1,398
Shumard oak	--	--	--	--	--	--	--	20	20	--	--	--	--	--	--	39
Other white oaks																
chestnut oak	--	--	59	117	196	235	235	137	59	59	20	--	--	--	--	1,115
post oak	--	--	--	--	20	100	--	--	39	--	--	--	--	--	--	159
Other red oaks																
scarlet oak	--	--	20	59	78	59	98	137	59	20	20	--	--	--	--	548
shingle oak	--	--	--	--	--	--	--	--	--	--	20	--	--	--	--	20
pin oak	--	--	--	--	--	--	--	--	--	--	20	--	--	--	--	20
black oak	1,219	487	334	176	59	157	98	98	176	78	137	--	--	--	--	3,019
Hickory																
bitternut hickory	--	--	--	59	39	59	--	39	39	--	--	--	--	--	--	235
pignut hickory	--	--	157	256	215	215	235	137	98	20	20	--	--	--	--	1,351
shagbark hickory	975	244	78	176	20	59	39	--	20	20	--	--	--	--	--	1,630
Hard maple																
sugar maple	13,195	3,673	1,496	965	671	316	176	157	98	20	--	20	--	--	--	20,786
Soft maple																
red maple	3,169	975	763	430	254	176	78	59	98	20	--	--	--	--	--	6,022
Beech																
American beech	7,069	1,219	215	274	78	59	--	59	--	59	20	20	--	--	--	9,070
Sweetgum																
sweetgum	--	--	--	--	20	--	--	--	--	--	--	--	--	--	--	20

(Table 3 continued on next page)

(Table 3 continued)

Species group							Diameter class (inches)										
	1.0-2.9	3.0-4.9	5.0-6.9	7.0-8.9	9.0-10.9	11.0-12.9	13.0-14.9	15.0-16.9	17.0-18.9	19.0-20.9	21.0-24.9	25.0-28.9	29.0-32.9	33.0-36.9	37.0+	All classes
Tupelo and blackgum																
blackgum	1,219	487	450	176	59	59	20	20	--	--	--	--	--	--	--	2,489
Ash																
white ash	2,437	244	294	198	215	137	78	20	39	20	--	--	--	--	--	3,682
green ash	--	--	--	--	--	20	--	--	--	--	--	--	--	--	--	20
Cottonwood and aspen																
bigtooth aspen	--	--	--	--	20	137	39	--	20	--	--	--	--	--	--	215
Yellow-poplar																
yellow-poplar	--	244	373	235	274	196	236	39	117	59	78	39	20	--	--	1,910
Black walnut																
black walnut	--	--	59	80	40	40	39	20	--	--	--	--	--	--	--	278
Other eastern soft hardwoods																
boxelder	--	--	--	39	--	--	--	--	--	--	--	--	--	--	--	39
European alder	--	--	20	--	--	--	--	--	--	--	--	--	--	--	--	20
river birch	--	--	--	--	20	20	--	--	--	--	--	--	--	--	--	39
hackberry	--	--	--	--	--	20	--	--	--	--	--	--	--	--	--	20
butternut	--	--	--	20	--	--	--	--	--	--	--	--	--	--	--	20
American sycamore	--	--	39	39	--	60	39	--	59	20	20	--	--	--	--	275
black cherry	487	731	215	98	20	78	20	--	--	20	--	--	--	--	--	1,649
sassafras	975	975	470	411	117	20	20	--	--	20	--	--	--	--	--	3,007
winged elm	2,437	244	59	39	78	20	20	--	--	--	--	--	--	--	--	2,779
American elm	975	748	176	78	78	20	20	--	--	--	--	--	--	--	--	2,094
Siberian elm	--	--	--	20	--	--	--	--	--	--	--	--	--	--	--	20
slippery elm	--	--	80	--	20	39	--	--	--	--	--	--	--	--	--	138
Other eastern hard hardwoods																
flowering dogwood	8,287	1,950	59	20	--	--	--	--	--	--	--	--	--	--	--	10,316
common persimmon	--	--	39	--	--	--	--	--	--	--	--	--	--	--	--	39
honeylocust	--	731	--	--	20	--	--	--	--	--	--	--	--	--	--	751
black locust	--	--	117	39	20	--	--	--	--	--	--	--	--	--	--	176
Eastern noncommercial hardwoods																
serviceberry spp	244	--	--	--	--	--	--	--	--	--	--	--	--	--	--	244
pawpaw	1,219	--	--	--	--	--	--	--	--	--	--	--	--	--	--	1,219
American hornbeam, musclewood	487	731	20	--	--	--	--	--	--	--	--	--	--	--	--	1,238
eastern redbud	504	1,008	99	--	--	--	--	--	--	--	--	--	--	--	--	1,611
eastern hophornbeam	2,681	--	20	--	--	--	--	--	--	--	--	--	--	--	--	2,701
All species groups	50,749	17,372	7,354	5,773	3,628	3,393	2,293	1,883	1,606	626	685	215	39	--	--	95,595

All table cells without observations in the inventory sample are indicated by --. Table value of 0 indicates the number of trees rounds to less than 1 thousand trees. Columns and rows may not add to their totals due to rounding.

Table 4.—Dry biomass of all live trees and standing dead trees on forest land by species and species group, Hoosier National Forest, Indiana, 2001-2005

(in thousand dry tons)

Species group	Live trees	Standing dead trees	All live and standing dead trees
Softwood species groups			
Loblolly and shortleaf pines			
shortleaf pine	493	16	508
Other yellow pines			
Virginia pine	28	--	28
Eastern white and red pines			
eastern white pine	269	45	313
Other eastern softwoods			
eastern redcedar	142	4	146
All softwoods	932	64	996
Hardwood species groups			
Select white oaks			
white oak	2,829	80	2,909
chinkapin oak	80	--	80
Select red oaks			
northern red oak	712	--	712
Shumard oak	41	--	41
Other white oaks			
chestnut oak	654	31	685
post oak	94	--	94
Other red oaks			
scarlet oak	390	36	426
shingle oak	39	--	39
pin oak	37	--	37
black oak	949	157	1,106
Hickory			
bitternut hickory	140	8	148
pignut hickory	766	--	766
shagbark hickory	175	--	175
Hard maple			
sugar maple	1,302	7	1,309
Soft maple			
red maple	501	--	501
Beech			
American beech	399	1	400
Sweetgum			
sweetgum	5	--	5
Tupelo and blackgum			
blackgum	107	2	109
Ash			
white ash	339	6	346
green ash	8	--	8
Cottonwood and aspen			
bigtooth aspen	84	--	84
Yellow-poplar			
yellow-poplar	880	42	922
Black walnut			
black walnut	70	1	71
Other eastern soft hardwoods			
boxelder	5	--	5
European alder	1	--	1

(Table 4 continued on next page)

(Table 4 continued)

Species group	Live trees	Standing dead trees	All live and standing dead trees
river birch	11	10	21
hackberry	8	--	8
butternut	2	2	4
American sycamore	190	--	190
black cherry	76	5	81
sassafras	153	19	172
winged elm	18	--	18
American elm	69	18	87
Siberian elm	2	--	2
slippery elm	21	2	23
Other eastern hard hardwoods			
flowering dogwood	52	1	53
common persimmon	2	--	2
honeylocust	11	--	11
black locust	14	--	14
Eastern noncommercial hardwoods			
serviceberry spp	1	--	1
pawpaw	4	--	4
American hornbeam, musclewood	11	--	11
eastern redbud	22	--	22
eastern hophornbeam	10	--	10
All hardwoods	11,281	427	11,708
All species groups	12,213	490	12,703

All table cells without observations in the inventory sample are indicated by - -. Table value of 0 indicates the aboveground tree biomass rounds to less than 1 thousand dry tons. Columns and rows may not add to their totals due to rounding.

Table 5.—Net volume of all live trees on forest land by species group and stand-size class, Hoosier National Forest, Indiana, 2001-2005

(in million cubic feet)

Species group	Stand-size class					All size classes
	Large diameter	Medium diameter	Small diameter	Chaparral	Nonstocked	
Loblolly and shortleaf pines	26 102.9	262.1	--	--	--	26 365.0
Other yellow pines	1 010.2	610.9	--	--	--	1 621.0
Eastern white and red pines	15 084.5	--	--	--	--	15 084.5
Other eastern softwoods	4 339.8	1 559.8	--	--	--	5 899.7
Select white oaks	97 333.4	1 337.3	116.8	--	--	98 787.6
Select red oaks	27 503.9	31.0	70.6	--	--	27 605.5
Other white oaks	24 911.7	160.8	--	--	--	25 072.5
Other red oaks	48 491.5	728.3	157.1	--	--	49 376.9
Hickory	36 236.1	78.6	319.7	--	--	36 634.5
Hard maple	37 607.5	2 276.0	84.3	--	--	39 967.8
Soft maple	16 206.2	2 436.7	33.2	--	--	18 676.2
Beech	11 937.3	--	--	--	--	11 937.3
Sweetgum	211.5	--	--	--	--	211.5
Tupelo and blackgum	3 749.2	--	--	--	--	3 749.2
Ash	11 538.9	780.7	56.8	--	--	12 376.5
Cottonwood and aspen	4 409.9	--	--	--	--	4 409.9
Yellow-poplar	39 515.5	6 172.3	88.1	--	--	45 775.9
Black walnut	2 713.6	101.4	--	--	--	2 815.0
Other eastern soft hardwoods	19 613.3	2 420.1	57.5	--	--	22 090.9
Other eastern hard hardwoods	556.4	387.5	--	--	--	943.9
Eastern noncommercial hardwoods	156.2	67.6	--	--	--	223.8
All species groups	429 229.7	19 411.3	984.3	--	--	449 625.3

All table cells without observations in the inventory sample are indicated by --. Table value of 0.0 indicates the volume rounds to less than 0.1 million cubic feet. Columns and rows may not add to their totals due to rounding.

Table 5a.—Net volume of all live trees on timberland by species group and stand-size class, Hoosier National Forest, Indiana, 2001-2005

(In million cubic feet)

Species group	Stand-size class					All size classes
	Large diameter	Medium diameter	Small diameter	Chaparral	Nonstocked	
Loblolly and shortleaf pines	20 668.4	262.1	- -	- -	- -	20 930.5
Other yellow pines	1 010.2	610.9	- -	- -	- -	1 621.0
Eastern white and red pines	15 084.5	- -	- -	- -	- -	15 084.5
Other eastern softwoods	4 339.8	1 559.8	- -	- -	- -	5 899.7
Select white oaks	90 182.7	1 337.3	116.8	- -	- -	91 636.9
Select red oaks	25 755.0	31.0	70.6	- -	- -	25 856.6
Other white oaks	19 399.2	160.8	- -	- -	- -	19 560.0
Other red oaks	45 494.3	728.3	157.1	- -	- -	46 379.6
Hickory	35 628.9	78.6	319.7	- -	- -	36 027.2
Hard maple	35 300.1	2 276.0	84.3	- -	- -	37 660.4
Soft maple	10 454.5	2 436.7	33.2	- -	- -	12 924.4
Beech	10 660.8	- -	- -	- -	- -	10 660.8
Sweetgum	211.5	- -	- -	- -	- -	211.5
Tupelo and blackgum	3 690.3	- -	- -	- -	- -	3 690.3
Ash	10 361.9	780.7	56.8	- -	- -	11 199.4
Cottonwood and aspen	4 409.9	- -	- -	- -	- -	4 409.9
Yellow-poplar	36 896.9	6 172.3	88.1	- -	- -	43 157.2
Black walnut	2 003.3	101.4	- -	- -	- -	2 104.7
Other eastern soft hardwoods	19 498.6	2 420.1	57.5	- -	- -	21 976.2
Other eastern hard hardwoods	556.4	387.5	- -	- -	- -	943.9
Eastern noncommercial hardwoods	156.2	67.6	- -	- -	- -	223.8
All species groups	**391 763.2**	**19 411.3**	**984.3**	**- -**	**- -**	**412 158.7**

All table cells without observations in the inventory sample are indicated by - -. Table value of 0.0 indicates the volume rounds to less than 0.1 million cubic feet. Columns and rows may not add to their totals due to rounding.

Table 6.—Net volume of sawtimber (International 1/4-inch rule) on timberland by species, species group, and diameter class, Hoosier National Forest, Indiana, 2001-2005

(In million board feet)[1]

Species group	Diameter class (inches)											All classes
	9.0-10.9	11.0-12.9	13.0-14.9	15.0-16.9	17.0-18.9	19.0-20.9	21.0-24.9	25.0-28.9	29.0-32.9	33.0-36.9	37.0+	
Softwood species groups												
Loblolly and shortleaf pines												
shortleaf pine	13	22	24	25	15	--	--	--	--	--	--	99
Other yellow pines												
Virginia pine	2	--	--	--	--	--	--	--	--	--	--	2
Eastern white and red pines												
eastern white pine	7	17	4	12	13	--	8	--	--	--	--	61
Other eastern softwoods												
eastern redcedar	3	2	5	2	3	--	--	--	--	--	--	15
All softwoods	25	41	33	39	31	--	8	--	--	--	--	178
Hardwood species groups												
Select white oaks												
white oak	--	35	49	88	62	41	63	26	11	--	--	374
chinkapin oak	--	3	--	--	7	--	--	--	--	--	--	10
Select red oaks												
northern red oak	--	5	7	10	21	17	15	35	--	--	--	111
Shumard oak	--	--	--	3	4	--	--	--	--	--	--	7
Other white oaks												
chestnut oak	--	17	23	14	7	6	6	--	--	--	--	74
post oak	--	7	--	--	8	--	--	--	--	--	--	15
Other red oaks												
scarlet oak	--	3	12	21	12	6	--	--	--	--	--	54
shingle oak	--	--	--	--	--	--	7	--	--	--	--	7
pin oak	--	--	--	--	--	--	6	--	--	--	--	6
black oak	--	12	8	14	37	21	49	--	--	--	--	142
Hickory												
bitternut hickory	--	5	--	7	9	--	--	--	--	--	--	21
pignut hickory	--	19	25	26	23	6	8	--	--	--	--	107
shagbark hickory	--	5	4	--	5	6	--	--	--	--	--	19
Hard maple												
sugar maple	--	27	20	25	14	6	--	--	--	--	--	92
Soft maple												
red maple	--	7	2	3	8	5	--	--	--	--	--	25
Beech												
American beech	--	--	--	--	--	13	9	--	--	--	--	22
Tupelo and blackgum												
blackgum	--	3	--	3	--	--	--	--	--	--	--	6
Ash												
white ash	--	8	10	--	10	6	--	--	--	--	--	33
Cottonwood and aspen												

(Table 6 continued on next page)

50

(Table 6 continued)

Species group	Diameter class (inches)											All classes
	9.0-10.9	11.0-12.9	13.0-14.9	15.0-16.9	17.0-18.9	19.0-20.9	21.0-24.9	25.0-28.9	29.0-32.9	33.0-36.9	37.0+	
bigtooth aspen	- -	11	5	- -	4	- -	- -	- -	- -	- -	- -	21
Yellow-poplar												
yellow-poplar	- -	17	34	8	30	15	47	28	19	- -	- -	199
Black walnut												
black walnut	- -	3	4	- -	- -	- -	- -	- -	- -	- -	- -	7
Other eastern soft hardwoods												
river birch	- -	1	- -	- -	- -	- -	- -	- -	- -	- -	- -	1
hackberry	- -	2	- -	- -	- -	- -	- -	- -	- -	- -	- -	2
American sycamore	- -	6	5	- -	16	6	9	- -	- -	- -	- -	42
black cherry	- -	4	2	- -	- -	- -	- -	- -	- -	- -	- -	6
sassafras	- -	2	2	- -	- -	6	- -	- -	- -	- -	- -	9
American elm	- -	2	- -	- -	- -	- -	- -	- -	- -	- -	- -	2
slippery elm	- -	3	- -	- -	- -	- -	- -	- -	- -	- -	- -	3
All hardwoods	- -	206	213	221	279	159	218	89	30	- -	- -	1 415
All species groups	25	247	246	260	310	159	226	89	30	- -	- -	1 592

All table cells without observations in the inventory sample are indicated by - -. Table value of 0 indicates the volume rounds to less than 1 million board feet. Columns and rows may not add to their totals due to rounding.
1 International 1/4-inch rule.

Table 7.—Average annual net growth of growing stock on forest land by species group and stand-size class, Hoosier National Forest, Indiana, 1999 and 2000 to 2004 and 2005

(In million cubic feet)

Species group	Stand-size class					All size classes
	Large diameter	Medium diameter	Small diameter	Chaparral	Nonstocked	
Loblolly and shortleaf pines	833.5	--	--	--	--	833.5
Other yellow pines	--	310.4	--	--	--	310.4
Other eastern softwoods	15.2	121.0	--	--	--	136.2
Select white oaks	2 196.0	259.7	--	--	--	2 455.6
Select red oaks	428.4	--	--	--	--	428.4
Other white oaks	170.0	25.0	--	--	--	195.0
Other red oaks	1 042.5	29.0	--	--	--	1 071.5
Hickory	1 104.9	11.8	--	--	--	1 116.7
Hard maple	1 344.8	133.8	--	--	--	1 478.6
Soft maple	-40.5	244.9	--	--	--	204.3
Beech	244.1	--	--	--	--	244.1
Tupelo and blackgum	74.6	--	--	--	--	74.6
Ash	66.5	19.4	--	--	--	85.9
Cottonwood and aspen	48.6	--	--	--	--	48.6
Yellow-poplar	1 377.6	14.3	--	--	--	1 391.9
Black walnut	70.6	46.0	--	--	--	116.6
Other eastern soft hardwoods	1 173.2	95.8	--	--	--	1 269.0
Other eastern hard hardwoods	18.0	129.0	--	--	--	147.0
All species groups	10 167.8	1 440.2	--	--	--	11 607.9

All table cells without observations in the inventory sample are indicated by --. Table value of 0.0 indicates the volume rounds to less than 0.1 million cubic feet. Columns and rows may not add to their totals due to rounding.

Table 7a.—Average annual net growth of growing stock on timberland by species group and stand-size class, Hoosier National Forest, Indiana, 1999 and 2000 to 2004 and 2005
(Note: table not included due to all estimates being identical to Table 7 for this national forest)

Table 8.—Average annual net removals of growing stock on forest land by species group and stand-size class, Hoosier National Forest, Indiana, 1999 and 2000 to 2004 and 2005
(Note: table not included due to all estimates being 0, no removals in national forest)

Table 8a.—Average annual net removals of growing stock on timberland by species group and stand-size class, Hoosier National Forest, Indiana, 1999 and 2000 to 2004 and 2005
(Note: table not included due to all estimates being 0, no removals in national forest)

Table 9.—Average annual mortality of growing stock on forest land by species group and stand-size class, Hoosier National Forest, Indiana, 1999 and 2000 to 2004 and 2005

(n million cubic feet)

| | Stand-size class | | | | | |
Species group	Large diameter	Medium diameter	Small diameter	Chaparral	Nonstocked	All size classes
Other yellow p nes	--	59 9	--	--	--	59 9
Other red oaks	1 101 8	--	--	--	--	1 101 8
Yellow-poplar	506 5	--	--	--	--	506 5
Other eastern soft hardwoods	137 1	--	--	--	--	137 1
Other eastern hard hardwoods	--	--	--	--	--	--
All species groups	1 745 4	59 9	--	--	--	1 805 3

All table cells without observations in the inventory sample are indicated by - . Table value of 0.0 indicates the volume rounds to less than 0.1 million cubic feet. Columns and rows may not add to their totals due to rounding.

Table 9a.—Average annual mortality of growing stock on timberland by species group and stand-size class, Hoosier National Forest, Indiana, 1999 and 2000 to 2004 and 2005
(Note: table not included due to all estimates being identical to Table 9 for this national forest)